MOLLY MEETS MONA AND FRIENDS

A magical day in the museum

Publisher's Cataloging-in-Publication
Provided by Quality Books, Inc.

Molly Meets Mona and Friends, a magical day in the Museum
Text copyright © 1997 by Gladys Walker. Illustrations copyright © 1997 by
Denise Bennett Minnerly. Typography by Alicia Mikles. All rights reserved including
the right of reproduction in whole or in part in any form. Printed in China.
For information address Greene Bark Press, PO Box 1108, Bridgeport, CT 06601

Library of Congress Cataloging in Publication Data
Walker, Gladys.
  Molly meets Mona and friends: a magical day in the museum / written by Gladys Walker;
story and illustrations by Denise Bennett.
      p.   cm.
  Preassigned LCCN: 97-71283
  ISBN 1-880851-25-3
    SUMMARY: A young girl who loves art spends a magical day in an art museum where
she imagines herself within many of the famous paintings of the European and American art
masters.
1. Museums–Juvenile fiction.   2. Art–Juvenile fiction.   I. Bennett, Denise.   II. Title.
PZ7.W355Mo 1997   [E]
                                        QBI97-40402

MOLLY MEETS MONA AND FRIENDS

A magical day in the museum

story and illustrations by DENISE BENNETT MINNERLY

text by GLADYS WALKER

GREENE BARK PRESS

Molly loves art. How she enjoys painting with the bright colors that squish out of her beautiful tubes of paint. She also likes to look at the paintings and sculpture by all the great artists of the world. When she's standing at her own easel, she feels like one of them! Today she needs some inspiration. Time to visit the art museum!

The museum is quiet except for the echo her shoes make as she climbs the wondrously wide marble staircase. *Click-click, click-click, click-click.*

She likes the paintings in gilded frames on the walls, from the giant-sized ones to the teeny tiny ones. "What will I discover today?" Molly wonders, as she skips off the top step and looks for the magical paintings down a long hallway.

A glow of light seems to be coming from a gigantic picture that's made of a zillion tiny dots of color. Some of the dots begin to whirl around Molly and draw her into the painting!

Everywhere people are strolling and picnicking and sailing in warm sunlight. "Is it a holiday?" she wonders. But no, she discovers, it's just *A Sunday On La Grande Jatte*, by impressionist, Georges Seurat. All of a sudden she takes off her hat and hands it to a tall gentleman promenading by with a lady on his arm. He takes the hat and nods his head gratefully. She hates to leave this pretty scene. But there's so much to see yet.

Click, click, click. Molly jaunts further down the hall and enters a large room. Suddenly the light dims and she finds herself standing in front of another painted landscape. But there are no picnickers here. It's John Constable's *Salisbury Cathedral from the Meadow.*

"It's dark and spooky," she thinks. "It looks stormy. Maybe I should have kept my hat!" she worries. She sees a church steeple pointing up to some shimmery clouds. And then she spies it . . . a beautiful rainbow! "The storm must be over!" Molly decides, as she delights in the misty ribbons of color. "I wonder where the rainbow ends . . ."

Molly skips merrily along until, suddenly, through the rainbow's display she sees furious white brush strokes that become churning clouds. "How different this sky looks from the other ones," she thinks. "How can it be the same sky?"

The clouds move so fast she has to leap higher and higher to catch up with them as she soars along right through Vincent Van Gogh's *Wheat Field and Cypress Trees.* Below her the bright yellow field sways this way and that. It's so dazzling she wishes she had worn her sunglasses! "How long have I been in the clouds?" she wonders. "It must be time to move on!"

Her feet hardly touch the marble floor again when Molly hears music. She prances on her tiptoes and follows the sound. Suddenly she comes upon the beautiful dancer in Edgar Degas' *Prima Ballerina.*

"What a gorgeous tutu! May I touch it?" she asks the ballerina, who motions her to dance. Molly raises her arms, and side by side gracefully they perform perfect pirouettes!

Just as they make their last turns, a strange sad sound drowns out the ballet music. Molly doesn't want to leave the ballerina, but she just has to find out what's going on.

Click . . . click . . . she takes only a few steps when from out of nowhere, something rushes at her! It's moving so fast, it's almost a blur. Now she recognizes the sound. It's the long low whistle of a train!

It's raining and Molly can barely see the train through the steamy fog, but somehow she manages to jump out of the way. Just in the nick of time! "I'm getting out while I can!" she declares, as she quickly runs away from *Rain, Steam And Speed–The Great Western Railway*, by Joseph Mallord William Turner.

"Whew! That was a close one!" Molly says aloud. The museum is quiet again as she turns a corner and starts down another hallway. *Click, click, click.* She stops in front of a large oil painting titled *More Than You Know*, by Elizabeth Murray.

"I wonder what it is?" Molly murmurs as she examines it. "I know it's not a train." She tips her head this way and that. Then she squints her eyes, and concentrates very hard.

All of a sudden she begins to see a table, some chairs, and other things. She stares at this abstract painting for a while. "It must be wonderful to be able to see things in a different way," she thinks. Finally she moves along.

Molly doesn't need to squint at the next picture. She knows right away that the people in this painting are telling an important story because it's *The Migration of the Negro*, by Jacob Lawrence.

She can tell by the suitcases and bundles the people are carrying, and by the determined way they're walking, that they're going somewhere. "But where?" Molly wonders. She walks on. "I need to ask someone about this." But before she can think of whom to ask, she gets a shivery feeling that someone is watching her.

Someone is! It's *Mona Lisa*! And she is smiling mysteriously at Molly! Molly has the feeling that she has seen her before. And she has! That's because the *Mona Lisa*, painted by Leonardo Da Vinci, is the most famous portrait in all the world.

In two giant leaps Molly sails past Mona. And all the while, Mona never takes her eyes off Molly. "What deep thoughts does she have?" Molly wonders. "I'll bet she knows the answers to everything!"

She doesn't have much time to think about this because she hears music again. But this time it's different.

Plink, plink, plink. "Who's playing that tune?" Molly wonders. She begins tapping merrily down the hall, and discovers *Three Musicians*, painted by Pablo Picasso.

Molly stares at the players. "Those must be guitars they're strumming," she decides, and she plays along with them. "I'm getting to like figuring things out!"

"The three musicians look like my paper dolls," she thinks. Everything in the painting has such sharp corners, that Molly wonders if her head and feet will begin to look like cubes, too, if she stands here too long!

But she doesn't have much time to think about this, because out of the corner of her eye she spies something very strange.

It's three little creatures sailing above her. "Wait for me!" Molly calls. She jumps up and catches one, and it carries her right into Wassily Kandinsky's *Sky Blue.*

More weird and wonderful creatures in bright colors are bobbing about everywhere. Molly floats in and out among them, trying to get a better look. "What are they?" she wonders. They're not like anything she's seen before. They give Molly such a free feeling that she decides they can be anything she wants them to be!

"What a glorious sky," she thinks. "The artist must love the color blue best of all. I may be in outer space. Maybe it's time to come back to earth."

Thud! Molly's toes touch the marble floor. But not for long. She takes two good leaps and balances herself on a giant lily pad floating in a shimmery pond. She has landed right in the middle of Claude Monet's wondrous *Water Lilies*.

"Peace and quiet . . . just what I need." Flowers drift along as far as she can see. Molly feels as if she's in a water garden. "Is this a dream?" she wonders. A gentle breeze carries her out among the blossoms. "What a lovely feeling!"

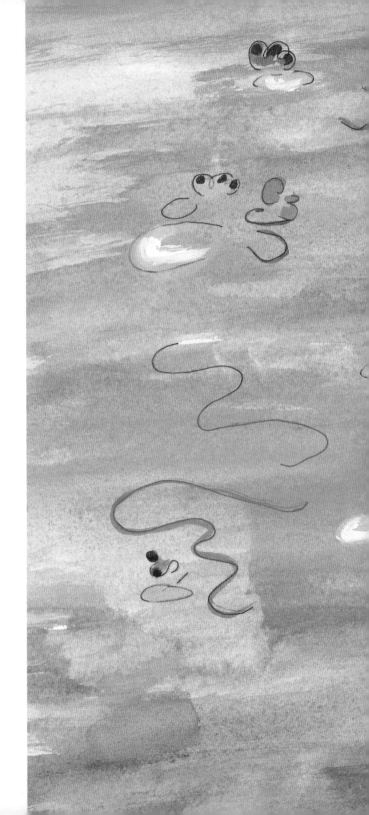

Squish, squish, squish. After her watery adventure Molly's toes leave tiny prints on the floor. But she soon forgets her wet feet, because–*thunk!*–she's busy balancing a coconut on her head! "What next," she wonders, as she follows the delicious smells of tropical fruit, right into Lois Mailou Jones' painting, *Les Vendeuses de Tissus.*

Here on the island of Haiti, women are carrying bolts of cloth on their heads, and holding up samples for buyers to admire.

The colors are shimmery in the bright island sunlight. "I wish I had a dress made of this cloth," Molly tells one of the women. But before the woman has a chance to speak, Molly realizes something is flying over her head. Is it a tropical bird?

Molly looks up very cautiously. "Oh, my!" It's Alexander Calder's *Lobster Trap And Fish Tail* mobile sculpture floating in midair.

The mobile drifts ever so slowly and Molly begins to feel a bit giddy. She closes her eyes, and when she opens them the mobile looks different. It has moved again!

Each time she closes and opens her eyes, it changes. Then she discovers that the mobile moves with the breezes. But it always stays balanced! "How does the artist get it to do that?!" she wonders. As she leaves, she walks backwards so that she can watch it change some more.

Although Molly hates to leave all her wonderful works of art, she knows it's time to go home. On the way out she waves to the tall man she saw in the very first painting she visited. "You can keep my hat!" she calls, and he nods to her once again.

Molly takes one last look back and waves. "Goodbye glorious art! See you again soon!" Her goodbye echoes down the corridor.

Then she skips to the top of the marble staircase and goes down the steps. *Click-click, click-click, click-click.* Out the front door.

Painting and Sculpture Credits